WORLD'S WEIRDEST SPORTS

Matt Roper

Matt Roper is a feature writer for British tabloid the *Daily Mirror*. He lived in Brazil for six years, where he managed to survive tarantula attacks, falling coconuts and swimming in piranha-infested waters in the Amazon jungle. He also infiltrated a Bolivian drug gang to investigate child prostitution rings, and dodged bullets to report on death squads in Rio de Janeiro. He returned to the UK after setting up a project for street girls in one of Brazil's biggest cities. He now lives in London with his wife Daniela.

He has written three other books, *Street Girls* and *Remember Me, Rescue Me*. In 2007 he wrote his first book for Penguin Books, *101 Crazy Ways to Die*.

WORLD'S

WEIRDEST

SPORTS

Matt Roper

PENGUIN BOOKS

PENGUIN BOOKS

Published by the Penguin Group

Penguin Group (NZ), 67 Apollo Drive, Rosedale,
North Shore 0632, New Zealand (a division of Pearson New Zealand Ltd)
Penguin Group (USA) Inc., 375 Hudson Street,
New York, New York 10014, USA
Penguin Group (Canada), 90 Eglinton Avenue East, Suite 700, Toronto,
Ontario, M4P 2Y3, Canada (a division of Pearson Penguin Canada Inc.)
Penguin Books Ltd, 80 Strand, London, WC2R 0RL, England
Penguin Ireland, 25 St Stephen's Green,
Dublin 2, Ireland (a division of Penguin Books Ltd)
Penguin Group (Australia), 250 Camberwell Road, Camberwell,
Victoria 3124, Australia (a division of Pearson Australia Group Pty Ltd)
Penguin Books India Pvt Ltd, 11, Community Centre,
Panchsheel Park, New Delhi - 110 017, India
Penguin Books (South Africa) (Pty) Ltd, 24 Sturdee Avenue,
Rosebank, Johannesburg 2196, South Africa

Penguin Books Ltd, Registered Offices: 80 Strand, London, WC2R 0RL, England

First published by Penguin Group (NZ), 2007
1 3 5 7 9 10 8 6 4 2

Copyright © Penguin Group (NZ), 2007

The right of Matt Roper to be identified as the author of this work in terms of
section 96 of the Copyright Act 1994 is hereby asserted.

Cover design by Renee Greenland
Internal design by Daniel Mesnage
Typeset by Egan Reid
Printed in Australia by McPherson's Printing Group

ISBN: 978 0 14 300754 8

A catalogue record for this book is available
from the National Library of New Zealand.

www.penguin.co.nz

CONTENTS

INTRODUCTION

Do you want to be a world-class player, but couldn't hit a ball if your life depended on it? Or maybe you dream of representing your country, but you're always the last to be picked for the Sunday morning kickaround?

Or do you just want to be the world's biggest sports fan, but you can't understand the offside rule, are completely baffled by rugby and don't know your zooters from your googlies?

Well, don't despair. There are plenty more sports out there, and although you might never have heard of them, they are played with just as much passion and get fans in just as much of a frenzy.

Forget football – trying to grab hold of a grease-smothered coconut can be just as much fun. And why play rugby, when you could be risking life and limb trying to pick up a headless goat carcass?

What is more exciting – trying to knock bails off stumps, or getting drunk while exploding packets of gunpowder?

We've tracked down the world's strangest sports, from the fascinating to the downright bizarre, from traditional games played for centuries to newfangled pastimes that are just catching on.

Once you know the rules to get you started, in no time at all you'll be fishing for squirrels in your local park, knocking a ball around with your buttocks, or pole-vaulting over canals.

With so many different sports to choose from, you're bound to be good at one of them. And, who knows, you might go down in history as one of the all-time greats.

So if you're fed up with being on the losing side and want something else to get your adrenalin pumping, turn the page . . .

GREASE WRESTLING

In the national sport of Turkey, men drenched in olive oil wrestle each other by putting their arms down their opponent's leather trousers and grabbing their crotch.

The sport, known as 'Yagly Gures', dates back to the Ottoman Empire. The annual three-day tournament in Kirkpinar, Turkey, has been held since 1362, making it the oldest continuously running sporting event in the world.

The wrestlers, known as 'pehlivan', meaning hero, wear a hand-stitched lederhosen made from water buffalo, which is often worn with suspenders. Only in 1975 was the duration of matches capped at 30 minutes – before this they used to go on for one or two days at a time until one wrestler established superiority.

Rules

Wrestlers must oil each other before an event as a demonstration of mutual respect. Wrestlers are not categorised by their weight, but by their knowledge and mastery of the sport. Victory is achieved when one wrestler either pins the other to the ground or lifts him above his shoulders.

Champion

The 2006 winner of the coveted golden belt and the title 'Head Wrestler of Turkey' was 22-year-old Osman Aynur, who successfully tackled his opponent's crotch in just eight minutes.

ULAMA

Rackets hadn't been invented when, 3500 years ago, the Aztecs wanted to knock a rubber ball around a court – so they used their buttocks and hips instead. The game, which is still played in parts of western Mexico, is one of the oldest continuously played sports in the world and is the oldest game to use a rubber ball.

The oldest ulama court, in the Mexican state of Chiapas, was built around 1500 BC, while latex balls have been carbon-dated to 500 years earlier. All but one of the game's rules have remained unchanged – the losers are no longer ritually sacrificed.

Rules

Ulama is played on a long, narrow court, called a taste, which is 60 metres long and only 4 metres wide. The opposing sides of five players each take turns serving the 4-kg (9-lb) rubber ball as they try to move the ball up the field, hitting it only with the buttocks or hip.

Points are scored if one team fails to return the other's serve across the halfway point, or if the serving team succeeds in getting the ball past the opponent's end line. The first team to score eight points wins. Games have been known to go on for up to seven days.

Champion

At just six years of age, Chuyito from Los Lanitos is the youngest – and one of the best – Ulama players in Mexico.

BA'

It's the world's roughest game, where players can kick, punch, head-butt, break down doors, smash windows, and even run through people's houses. The ancient game of Ba' (Orkney Scots for 'ball') is played twice a year, on Christmas Day and New Year's Day, in the town of Kirkwall in the Scottish Orkney Isles.

Two teams, the Uppies, who live on the north side of town, and the Doonies, who live on the south, battle to gain control of the Ba', a 1.4-kg (3-lb) leather ball. Games can go on for many hours and injuries include concussion, crushed ribs and broken legs.

The wild game is supposed to have started a thousand years ago when two groups of Vikings started kicking around the decapitated head of a hated enemy. They had so much fun that they made it into a sport.

Rules

The Doonies have to dunk the Ba' in the water of Kirkwell's harbour to win, while the Uppies have to touch it on a wall in the south end of town. There are no referees and no penalties, and each team can have as many players as they want – usually about 300.

Champion

The last two games were won by the Uppies, but overall the winners' table is pretty evenly split. The person who scores the win has the honour of keeping the Ba' for a year, but he also has the entire team round to his place for refreshments.

EXTREME IRONING

There are now thousands of extreme ironing devotees who like nothing more than taking the creases out of their clothes halfway up cliffs, or while skiing down a mountainside, or even while under water.

The sport was invented by Briton Phil Shaw (known in the ironing world as 'Steam'), who in 1997 came home from work to a pile of ironing, wishing he could go rock climbing instead – so decided to do both at the same time.

The first Extreme Ironing World Championships took place near Munich, Germany, in 2002. Teams of 'ironists' were tested with five arduous ironing tests on a variety of fabrics and in different environments, ranging from rocky to forest, urban, and water, including a fast-flowing river.

Rules

You can iron anywhere except indoors. Boards must be at least 1.5 metres (5 feet) long and have legs, and the garment being ironed must be at least tea-towel-sized. The iron must be switched on, calling for a very long extension cord or power generator.

Champion

American wrestler Adam Pearce was awarded the coveted title of 'Champion of the Universe' in November 2006, after he launched himself from a plane at 7625 metres (25,000 feet), then firmly pressed a shirt, the trousers he was wearing, a pair of wrestling tights, and his parachute (which he repacked in mid-air) before landing safely five minutes later.

KABADDI

It might involve players holding their breath while dashing around in their underwear, but Kabaddi is as popular a sport in India as football is in Brazil. In fact, the game, which to the uninitiated looks like tag for adults, rouses millions of people to a fanatical frenzy all over Asia.

Teams take turns to send one of their seven players into the opponents' court to try to touch as many opposing players as possible in one breath, and before having to take another breath. Meanwhile, the defending team try to grab and hold him until he has to take another breath.

The team sport began 4000 years ago as a way to develop the physical strength, speed and skill of young warriors. Tournaments are now held around the world, and the sport was even included in the Asian Games in Beijing in 1990.

Rules

Each match has two halves lasting 20 minutes each. Points are scored by touching or catching the opposing team's players. Once a player is touched, or if the attacking player takes a breath while in the opponents' court, they are out. While they are in their opponents' court, attacking players must shout 'Kabaddi, Kabaddi . . .' to prove they are not breathing.

Champion

The Pele of the Kabaddi world is Balwinder Phiddu, a player from Punjab who retired after the 1997 World Cup, following a career spanning 22 years. He is considered a national hero in India and is believed to have made vast amounts of money.

SQUIRREL FISHING

Once you've hooked a squirrel, you'll never cast your line into a lake or river ever again. So say the growing number of squirrel fishing devotees, a rapidly growing (but surprisingly humane) sport that has become especially popular on American university campuses.

The pastime, which started as a research project by students at Harvard University, involves lifting squirrels into the air using a peanut or other bait tied to a string or fishing line. Perfecting the delicate art takes months of practice and also involves learning how to speak 'squirrel', which apparently helps put the rodents at ease.

Rules

Once the squirrel grabs on to the bait, the fisher must gently lift it fully off the ground. Squirrels must not be harmed or overfed. Once caught, they must be given the nut as a reward and sent on their way.

Champion

There haven't been any official squirrel fishing contests as yet, but if there were, the winner would probably be a member of the Berkeley Squirrel Fishers' Association, the world's biggest university squirrel fishing club, with over 80 members.

BUZKASHI

The national sport of Afghanistan, Buzkashi is played on horseback and literally means 'goat grabbing'. The sport is often compared to polo – except that goals are scored, not with a ball, but with a headless goat carcass.

Serious Buzkashi players train intensively for years, and many of the masters – called 'chapandaz' – are over 40 years old. The games sometimes go on for days and can be extremely violent, with as many as 500 players battling to gain control of the carcass. The game ends with a spot of wrestling – if there's anyone still standing.

Variations on the game include a free-for-all, in which individual riders compete alone, and 'dara-yi-Buzkashi', which is played in the middle of a river and often ends up with one or two players drowning.

Rules

Players battle to pick up the carcass and drop it into the scoring circle or over the goal line. Riders are not allowed to hit other opponents on the hand, but punching, whipping and kicking is allowed. Women are not allowed to watch.

TEJO

Despite involving an apparently dangerous combination of alcohol, flying metal and gunpowder, the traditional sport of Colombia boasts a surprisingly low casualty rate.

The game involves lobbing a 2-kg (4.4-lb) metal plate ('tejo') at packets filled with gunpowder – with the aim of making them explode – while downing copious amounts of beer or aguardiente, an aniseed-flavoured firewater.

The sport was first played 500 years ago by the indigenous Chibcha tribes using pure gold discs. One Indian chief who wanted to become a Roman Catholic apparently made his seven wives play Tejo and abandoned all but the winner.

Rules

Small envelopes filled with gunpowder called 'mechas' are placed on the edges of a metal ring in a box filled with clay. Teams take turns to throw the tejo, hoping to make contact with the metal ring and make the mechas explode. The team that makes the most explosions wins, while the losers have to pick up the bar bill.

URBAN GOLF

Urban golfers have more than bunkers to worry about – their balls are often swept up by street cleaners, lost down drains or carried off by stray dogs. Essentially normal golf played in an urban environment, the game involves players using skyscrapers to tee off, the street as a fairway, and bins, skips or water hydrants as a hole to putt into.

The sport began in 2004, when London-based golfer Jeremy Feakes got sick of snobbery at his local golf course and took to the streets, car parks and open spaces of East London. He later formed the first 18-hole, par-72 urban golf open with the slogan: 'Go Play in the Traffic'.

Urban golf is now played in the streets of cities around the world with thousands of devoted players. Campus Golf has also sprung up on university campuses, while in Australia the game has two variations – play to the pub, or to the beach.

Rules

A leather ball stuffed with goose feathers is used so nothing gets damaged. Private property is out of bounds. Players are allowed to tee off a mat rather than hit the ball off a pavement, and balls can be dropped a club's length away from any object that interferes with your swing.

LAND DIVING

If the thought of bungy jumping sends you into a cold sweat, then spare a thought for the people of the South Pacific island Pentecost, who throw themselves off a 25-metre (82-feet) -high tower with just vines tied to their ankles. Men and boys as young as seven participate in the annual ritual, which is supposed to prove their manhood and ensure a good harvest.

It is said to have evolved from the story of a woman who spent years trying to escape the unwanted attentions of her husband. In desperation, she climbed a tall tree and threatened to leap to her death, daring her husband to follow her if his love was true. The wily wife had tied vines to her ankles, which saved her, but the husband leapt to his death.

Seconds before jumping, the diver tells the crowd his most intimate thoughts, just in case they are his last words. Yet only one land diver is known to have died, during a visit by Queen Elizabeth II in 1974 – during the dry season, when the vines are drier and less elastic. The ancient ritual is also said to have inspired the modern-day thrill sport bunjy jumping, which has actually claimed far more lives.

Rules

The diver's head is meant to touch the ground to fertilise it. The diver selects his own vines, which in itself is a fine art, as if they are too long he can crush his skull, and if they are too short bones can be broken as he is jerked back into the tower. Men wear a penis sheath while women dance below wearing grass skirts.

COMPETITIVE EATING

If you're no good at running, but can scoff a plate of nachos in 30 seconds flat, then you're apparently no less of an athlete. Eating unimaginable amounts of food in the shortest time possible is a growing competitive sport, especially in Japan and the US, where contests are regularly aired on sports channels.

You name it, there's a competition for eating it – from hotdogs to hard-boiled eggs, cow brains to burritos, oysters, mayonnaise and even butter. Heavyweights include Bill 'El Wingador' Simmons, who once ate 137 chicken wings in 30 minutes, and Sonya 'The Black Widow' Thomas, who ate 65 hard-boiled eggs in under seven minutes.

Rules

Eaters must be over 18. Competitions are judged by the amount eaten within a set period of time, usually 10 or 12 minutes. Contestants can eat the food however they want and are allowed to dip it into water to make it softer. Vomiting means instant disqualification.

Champion

The reigning champion of worldwide eating is Takeru 'The Tsunami' Kobayashi. He holds the world record for hotdog eating – 53¾ hotdogs in 12 minutes in July 2006. Despite only weighing 73 kg (160 lb), he has also scoffed 97 burgers in eight minutes and 8 kg (18 lb) of cow brains in 15 minutes.

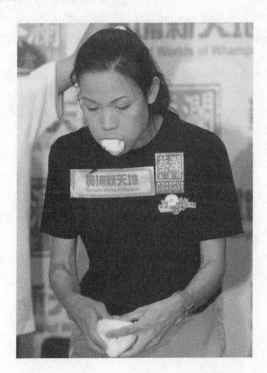

WIFE CARRYING

Men in Finland used to court women by running into their village, picking them up, and carrying them off. Today they do it in the more conventional (and time-consuming) way, with wife carrying now being a competitive sport practised around the world.

The best husbands get to carry their wives off to the world championships in Sonkajavi, Finland, where the winner's prize is his wife's weight in beer. There is also a wife-carrying relay, where three men carry the same wife in turns, and a wife-carrying triathlon, which includes carrying your wife while riding a bike.

Rules

The course is 235.5 metres (772.6 feet) long with two dry obstacles and a 1-metre (3 feet) -deep water obstacle. The wife may be your own, or your neighbour's, but she must be over 17 years of age and weigh at least 49 kg (108 lb). If the contestant drops his wife, the couple is fined 15 seconds.

Champion

Estonian Margo Uusong lugged wife Sandra Kullas to the finish line in a record 56.9 seconds in 2006, much to the dismay of the Finns who have been wife-carrying for centuries.

NOL-TTWIGI

It looks just like a playground seesaw, but don't expect to get gently rocked up and down. In this traditional Korean pastime, participants must try to propel their partner as far into the air as possible by jumping on their side of the seesaw as hard as they can.

Noi-Ttwigi is played mostly by women during traditional holidays and festivals. It is said to have originated during a time when a woman's place was firmly within the home. Women would use the seesaws to propel themselves high enough over the walls of the family compound to catch a glimpse of the world outside.

Rules

A thick plank of wood, about 3.3 metres (10.8 feet) long, is balanced on top of a rolled-up sheaf of straw or straw bag. One woman stands on each end of the plank and each take turns to jump up and land on the board, making the other fly upwards. The aim is to fly as high into the air as possible, with extra points for acrobatics and somersaults. The game finishes when one of the women falls off.

CHESS BOXING

Here's a sport where you can have a left jab one minute, a pawn-taking bishop the next, and a right hook straight after that. Chess boxing consists of 11 alternating rounds of chess and boxing, and aims to combine the physical exertion of one sport with the mental challenge of the other.

Players win either by a knockout in the ring or checkmate on the board. With no break between each round, players must keep their wits about them, even if they've just taken a battering in the ring. The game was first played in 2003 in Berlin, Germany, and now eagerly anticipated contests are held around the world.

Rules

The chess board is placed in the middle of the boxing ring. There are six rounds of chess, each lasting four minutes, and five of boxing, each lasting two minutes. The rounds take place alternately, beginning and ending with chess, with one-minute intervals. In the event of a draw in the chess and no knockout, a points winner can be declared on the basis of performance in the ring.

Champion

The current world champion is Frank 'Anti-Terror' Stolt, who beat Zoran 'The Priest' Mijatovic in Cologne, Germany, in 2006.

BOG SNORKELLING

For most people snorkelling means exploring the crystal clear waters of a tropical reef – not flapping about in the icy cold mud of a peat bog. Yet every August hundreds of people descend on the smallest village in Britain, Llanwrtyd Wells in Wales, to do just that.

The annual Bog Snorkelling World Championships have become so successful since the sport was invented in 1986 that spin-offs now include mountain bike bog snorkelling, in which the tyres are filled with water and the bike frame with lead, and the bog snorkelling triathlon.

Rules

Contestants must swim two lengths in the fastest time possible of a 50-metre (60-yard) trench, cut 1-metre (4-feet) deep through the peat bog. Entrants wear snorkels and flippers and must not use conventional swimming strokes. Whoever completes the course in the quickest time wins a year's supply of 'mudslide' flavour ice cream.

Champion

The bog snorkelling world record holder is Phillip John, of Bridgend, who powered through the mud in just 1 min 35 seconds in 1993.

SLAMBALL

This is a version of basketball where players try to pull off high-flying slam-dunks after launching themselves off trampolines.

It was first played in Los Angeles after founder Mason Gordon decided he wanted to create a sport that resembled a video game. The spring-loaded court is enclosed with Plexiglas walls so the ball is always in play, and each team has a 'stopper', whose job it is to do whatever possible to stop the other team from scoring, leading to spectacular mid-air collisions.

Slamball made its television debut in 2002 and now has its own league and millions of fans.

Rules

There are four players from each team on the court at any one time. Full body contact is allowed in mid-air, so players can push, hit and block their opponents to prevent them scoring. Slam-dunks and shots behind the arc are worth three points. All other baskets are worth two.

PARKOUR

An ideal sport for people who want to get home in time for their favourite soap, parkour is the art of getting from A to B as quickly and efficiently as possible, using the abilities of the human body.

Started in France in the 1990s, the sport combines elements of rock climbing and martial arts to 'flow' over obstacles in your path, while always remaining in motion. In a city, that might mean scaling walls, running over roofs, or even jumping from one building to the next.

Although the sport is relatively unknown, you've probably seen parkour in films and television commercials. The opening chase scene in the James Bond movie *Casino Royale*, for example, features parkour founder David Belle as a terrorist running along rooftops, chased by 007.

Rules

Parkour participants, called 'traceurs', must move as fast as they can, but in a way that is the least energy-consuming and at the same time the most direct. Good jumping and landing techniques, such as the roll after a drop, are important to avoid injury and remain in motion.

Champion

The first parkour world championship were held in 2007 in Munich, Germany.

TODD RIVER REGATTA

What, you may ask, is so weird about a boat race held every year on the Todd River in Alice Springs, central Australia? Well, nothing, if it weren't for the fact that the river is almost perpetually dry. In fact, the nearest body of water is nearly 1609 kilometres (1000 miles) away.

Determined not to let such a minor inconvenience ruin their regatta, competitors stick their legs through the bottom of their boats and run along the sandy riverbed to the finish line. The event has now being going for 46 years and was only cancelled once – because the river flooded – in 1993.

Rules

Races include eights, fours, kayaks, an armada of other offbeat boats such as submarines and pirate ships, and the ever popular four-men-carrying-a-woman-in-a-bathtub.

CAMEL WRESTLING

Apparently camels are natural wrestlers. When a female's at stake, the males fight by trying to trip each other up using their legs and bodies, leaning on them to topple them over, or even getting their opponent in a lock and sitting on top of him.

In Turkey, where camel wrestling championships draw thousands of spectators, there are an estimated 1200 specially bred animals, called 'tulu'. The camels wrestle with others in their same weight class, and each has a different trick or special skill to outwit their opponent.

However, the best part of a tournament is when one of the camels makes a break for it and charges into the crowd, sending them running for their lives. Another peril for spectators is the camel slobber that tends to be sprayed around, and the fact they are one of the few animals who can projectile urinate – backwards.

Rules

Two camels are prepared for wrestling after a female in heat is led past them. For a winner to be declared, one of the camels has to run out of the arena, cry out of frustration after being dominated by the opponent, or fall to the ground. The owner of a camel may also throw a rope into the field to declare a forfeit if he is concerned for the safety of his animal.

BOSSABALL

There can't be many other sports that combine volleyball, football, gymnastics, trampolining and samba. In Bossaball, two teams try to volley the ball over a net, while flinging themselves around on what looks like a giant bouncy castle.

While the inflatable court allows for mid-air bicycle kicks and diving digs, the two big trampolines in the centre mean that players can propel themselves 4.5 metres (15 feet) in the air, leading to spectacular smashes. The game is also often played to Brazilian samba rhythms, with referees doubling as DJs and equipped with a set of drums and a mixing deck, as well as a whistle.

While the game looks and sounds as though it came straight from the beaches of Rio, it was developed in Belgium and is played mostly in Spain.

Rules

Bossaball is played between two teams of either three, four or five people. Any body part can be used and each team is allowed up to eight touches before returning the ball. Points are won for grounding the ball on the opponents' side, one point if it lands on the inflatables, and three points on the trampoline.

VERTICAL MARATHON

For thousands of athletes, winning the vertical marathon is the high point – literally – of their careers. This is not the best sport for vertigo-sufferers. The aim of the game is to reach the top of some of the world's tallest buildings in the quickest time possible.

The first vertical marathon was held in Singapore in May 1987, when 130 men and 50 women climbed the 1336 steps and 73 floors of the Stamford Hotel, which at the time was the world's highest hotel. The race now attracts thousands of competitors, and similar competitions have sprung up all over the world, including the 1576 steps and 86 floors of the Empire State Building.

Rules

Runners are sent up the stairwell in batches of three at a time, at one-minute intervals. Anyone who blocks, pushes or shoves other participants is disqualified. The runner who reaches the finish line on the top of the building first is the winner. They are allowed to take the lift back down.

Champion

No runner has yet managed beat the record set by Singaporean Balvinder Singh, who flew up the Stamford Hotel in six minutes 55 seconds in 1989.

FIERLJEPPEN

The traditional Dutch sport of canal vaulting is believed to have originated from farmers who used poles to jump quickly over water drainage channels to get to the next field.

The vaulters, or 'fierljeppers', dive off a launch pad to catch a long aluminium pole, which they use to propel themselves across the canal while shimmying to the top of it, with the aid of bicycle inner tubes strapped to their feet. Then, just before the pole hits the other side of the canal, they leap as far as they can into a sand pit.

Rules

Before the jump, the pole has to be placed at the right distance from the platform. After a 20-metre (66-feet) sprint, the jumper must grab the pole with both arms and swing their legs both sides of it. The vaulter who jumps the furthest distance wins.

Champion

The current world record is held by Bart Hemholt, who jumped a massive 9 metres 48 centimetres (26 feet 19 inches) in 2006.

DWARF TOSSING

Perhaps the least politically correct pastime of all time, this involves grabbing a little person and hurling him as far as you can.

The sport began in pubs in Australia, where the first Dwarf Tossing World Championships were held in 1986. The most aerodynamic little people, who wear crash helmets and specially padded suits, can earn as much as US$100,000 (NZ$135,136) a year.

Dwarf tossing has been banned in France and in several US states, including Florida, where bars holding contests can have their liquor licence revoked. In Ontario, Canada, the Dwarf Tossing Ban Act 2003 means anyone caught throwing dwarfs can face around a CA$5000 (NZ$6000) -dollar fine or six months in prison.

Rules

As well as protective knee and elbow padding, the dwarf wears a harness fitted with a handle on the back. Throwers take turns to toss the dwarf from behind a white line onto a pile of mattresses. The person who throws the furthest wins a cash prize or trophy.

Champion

The longest dwarf toss on record was during the British Dwarf Tossing championships of 2002, when Jimmy Leonard of England tossed all 44 kg (98 lb) of Lenny the Giant an impressive 3.5 metres (11 feet 5 inches).

OSTRICH RACING

Ostriches can run at speeds of up to 80 kilometres an hour (50 mph). But the big birds that compete in races in parts of northern Africa have an extra incentive to be the fastest – when the race is over the losers are eaten.

Jockeys either ride 'featherback' by holding onto the bird's wings, or in two-wheeled chariots, using sticks to push the birds' heads in one direction or the other.

However, ostriches are pretty unpredictable and tend to run in any direction they feel like, making for a hilarious spectator sport, as jockeys hang on to the gangly two-legged birds for dear life. Only the most experienced riders manage to stay on for more than a few seconds.

Rules

The first ostrich across the finish line with the jockey still riding is the winner. Most races are over 400 metres (1312 feet), but as there is no way of stopping an ostrich once it starts running, ostrich and rider could end up anywhere.

CHEESE ROLLING

For most people, a cheese roll doesn't mean tumbling 274 metres (300 yards) down a near vertical slope in pursuit of a 3-kg (7-lb) round of Double Gloucester. But hundreds of people risk life and limb to do just that in this annual event, believed to be one of England's oldest sports.

Held every May on Cooper's Hill, Gloucestershire, which has a gradient of 2:1 for most part and 1:1 in places, it started as a pagan festival to celebrate the start of summer – a fact probably lost on the dozens who find themselves in the back of an ambulance every year. One year, the round of cheese, which hurtles down the hill at 133 kilometres an hour (70 mph), even struck a spectator on the head, sending him tumbling into A&E.

Rules

There are three races where a 7-cm (3-inch) -thick wheel of cheese is rolled downhill, chased five seconds later by twenty contestants at a time. The first person to pass the finish line at the bottom wins the cheese they are chasing after. Rugby players wait at the bottom to tackle anyone still running to prevent them crashing into a fence.

Champion

Local man Stephen Gyde, 43, holds the record for the most races won – a total of 21. He is also the only competitor to have won all three races in a single year, twice.

YUBI LAKPI

Literally translated as 'coconut snatching', this traditional Indian game involves grabbing a coconut smeared in grease and holding on to it for dear life while sprinting down a field.

The aim is to carry the slippery coconut to a rectangular box area at one end of the field, then over the goal line, without being dispossessed by the opposing team. The scorer must then dedicate his coconut to the 'king' – now the judge – who sits just beyond the goal line.

As if grabbing a lubricated coconut wasn't hard enough, players are regularly doused with water from a hose to make the task even more difficult. If no player succeeds in getting their nut to the 'king', all the players are lined up and made to a run a race to decide the victor.

Rules

Each team contains seven players. The game starts when the referee lobs the coconut into the centre of the field. Players must penetrate the box area from the front, not from the sides. Kicking the coconut is not allowed.

ETON WALL GAME

A sport only for those rich, posh or brainy enough to attend the elite, boys-only Eton College, the Wall Game has been played every St Andrew's Day since 1776. The big fixture is played between a team of 'Collegers' (scholarship holders – the brainy ones) and a team of 'Oppidans' (the rest of the students – the rich/posh ones).

It is played on a 5-metre (16-feet) strip that runs the length of a straight 110-metre (120-yard) wall on the school premises, and the game starts when the Oppidans climb over the wall after throwing their caps over in defiance of the scholars. The rules are obscure and while the aim of the game is to score goals, the last goal was scored in 1909.

Rules

Each team tries to move the ball towards their opponents' end of the playing area. In those last few yards of the field a player can earn a 'shy' (worth one point) by lifting the ball against the wall with his foot. Players are not allowed to handle the ball and can't touch the ground with anything other than their hands and feet. A goal (worth nine points) is scored by throwing the ball at a designated target – a garden door at one end of the field and a tree at the other.

CANNONBALL RUN

This is a cross-country, and often cross-continent, car rally held on public roads where drivers race to cross the finish line first – without getting arrested for speeding.

Some races last for days or even weeks and cover thousands of kilometres, often including ferry crossings. While organisers advise against breaking the speed limit, drivers can use 'any means possible' to win – which often means taking short cuts to dodge police road-blocks and using laser jammers to disable speed cameras.

The sport is named after American racer Edwin G 'Cannonball' Baker, who died a hero in 1960 after setting 143 cross-country records, including a 53½-hour coast-to-coast drive averaging 53 mph (85 kilometres an hour) in 1933. The first race held in his honour was the Cannonball Baker Sea-to-Shining-Sea Memorial Trophy Dash in 1971, in defiance of a newly introduced 55 mph (88 kilometres an hour) speed limit.

Rules

Whoever makes the fastest overall time is the winner. Drivers can use any route they like to reach the destination. Being pulled over by the police or having your car impounded doesn't mean disqualification, it just slows you down.

Champion

The 2006 European winners were Stuart Heade and Josie Thompson, who drove the 4828 kilometres (3000 miles) from Surrey, England, through Italy and France to Brussels, Belgium, with an average speed of 98.14 kilometres an hour (60.98 mph).

CALCIO STORICO

It might look like a pitch invasion by football hooligans in fancy dress, but Calcio Storico is an ancient game played since Roman times in Florence, Italy – although players often seem less bothered about scoring goals and more preoccupied with beating each other to a pulp.

Wearing medieval garters and pantaloons, players must seize the ball and put it into the goal, which runs the entire width of the playing field. The game is played on a giant sand pit, to soak up the blood as players punch, trip and kick their opponents – whether they've got the ball or not.

And what do the winners get for putting themselves through it? A pile of steaks of a weight equivalent to that of a white calf, which was historically butchered for the occasion.

Rules

Four teams of 27 players participate in the tournament, each representing one of Florence's four traditional neighbourhoods. Each game is played out for 50 minutes, with the winner being the team that has scored the most goals. Any means possible can be used to stop the opposing team advancing.

HURLING

Don't worry, this isn't a vomiting competition. In fact, hurling is one of Ireland's most popular sports and is arguably the fastest – and most dangerous – field sport in the world, with balls propelled through the air at speeds of up to 161 kilometres an hour (100 mph).

To the outsider it's like a mad kind of aerial hockey, where players use wooden axe-shaped sticks called 'hurleys' to hurtle a pellet-hard ball called a 'sloitar' between the opponents' goalposts. With the ball travelling at breakneck speeds and players swinging their sticks wildly, injuries are common – around a thousand people are admitted to Cork hospital with hurling-related injuries every year.

The game dates back to the fifth century, when, according to legend, ancient Irish warrior Cúchulainn used a hurley and a well-aimed sloitar to kill a ferocious wild dog.

Rules

Each team has 15 players and they play on a pitch about 150 yards (137 metres) long and 90 yards (82 metres) wide. They may propel the ball by hitting it with their hands, feet or hurleys, but they may not throw it. A goal is worth three points, and one point is awarded for hitting the ball over the bar and between the posts. Physical contact is essential to the game, but holding or rugby tackling is not allowed.

Champion

Still considered the greatest hurling player of all time, Christy Ring won a record eight All-Ireland Senior Hurling Championships for Cork during the 1940s, 1950s and 1960s. When he died suddenly aged 58 in 1979, over 60,000 people attended his funeral.

MAN VERSUS HORSE

Four legs against two might not seem very fair, but every year hundreds of runners from around the world compete against horses and riders in this annual, long-distance race in Llanwrtyd Wells, Wales.

The event started in 1980 after the landlord of the local pub got into a heated discussion with a customer about the chances of man against horse. Maintaining – after a few pints – that a man could outrun a horse over long distances, he offered £1000 (NZ$2,699) to the first person to do it.

The first race attracted 40 runners and six horses – and a horse won. In fact, 25 years later the landlord was still trying to prove his point, by which time the prize money had risen to £25,000 (NZ$67,492).

Rules

Runners and horses with riders race along the same 22-mile (35-kilometre) course, through fields and marshland. Various cash prizes are awarded to the first horse, runner and relay team to finish. While relay teams have managed to beat the horse occasionally, only individual runners can collect the big prize money.

Champion

In 2004, Londoner Huw Lobb made history by beating 47 horses and 500 other human runners to the finish line and scooping £25,000 (NZ$67,492) – one of the biggest unclaimed prizes in British athletics.

JAI-ALAI

Jai-Ali is the world's fastest ball game – and also one of the most dangerous, with rock-hard balls travelling at speeds of more than 290 kilometres an hour (180 mph). With crippling and even fatal injuries common among players, not getting hit by a ball is a matter of life and death.

The game began 300 years ago in Spain's Basque region, where a boy with a broken arm, who wanted to join his friends in a game of catch, used a broken basket to throw and catch the ball. Players strap on a 70-centimetre (28-inch) -long wicker basket scoop to their wrist, which they use to hurl the 125-g (4-oz) leather ball at a granite wall.

Rules

The court has three walls and players have to hit the front wall with the ball, using enough speed and spin so that the opponent cannot catch or return it. Points are awarded when an opponent can't return or puts the ball out of bounds. Usually played in pairs or in teams of three, the first team to nine points wins.

Champion

The undisputed world champion is Francisco Maria Churruca Iriondo Azpiazu Alcorta, known to his friends as Patxi.

SHIN KICKING

Shin kicking has been played in England and Wales for over four centuries. It was once taken so seriously that competitors would harden their shins by hitting them with coal hammers.

Back then, shin kickers would sometimes fight stark naked and wear boots tipped with iron, which would often leave participants crippled for life. Today competitors are allowed to stuff their trousers with straw – although it doesn't do much to lessen the pain.

The Skin Kickers Association of Britain, appropriately named SKAB, is now campaigning to have the sport included in the 2012 Olympics in London. Their motto – 'If it ain't broken, yer not kickin' hard enough.'

Rules

Participants square up like wrestlers, each holding the other's collar, with the aim of bringing the opponent to the ground solely by means of applying foot to foreleg. Kickers who topple their opponents two out of three times go through to the next round. In the event that both men fall, the last one to hit the ground wins. A 'stickler', the ancient name for a judge or umpire, is on hand to make sure a shin is hit before a fall can be scored.

Champion

The 2006 Shin Kicking Championship was won by Steve Preston, also known as 'Stupid Steve'.

CASTELL

The traditional sport of human tower building has been practised in the Catalonian region of Spain for centuries. Teams of 'castellers' practise all year round to compete at festivals to build the highest and most impressive structures.

Some towers can reach 10 storeys high and are only complete when a small child, called the 'enxaneta' and almost always a girl, clambers to the very top and raises their hand with four fingers erect – to represent the stripes of the Catalonian flag.

Towers often collapse before they are completed, and injuries are common as the castellers topple into the crowd below them. In 2006, a 12-year-old girl climbing to the top of a 10-storey tower fell off and died.

Rules

A castell is considered a success when it is properly assembled and dismantled. Castellers usually go barefoot and wear a sash to give others a foothold when climbing up.

UNDERWATER RUGBY

This is described as the world's only 3D sport, as the field of play is a 5-metre (16-feet) -deep swimming pool and players can pass in any direction – up and down as well as side to side.

Despite the name, however, it has little in common with normal rugby. There are no scrums or tries, the teams are mixed sex, and the goal is a heavy metal bucket on the bottom of each end of the pool. The ball is filled with salt water, to make it slightly heavier than the pool water, so it can be flung under water.

The game was first played in 1964 in Mülheim, Germany, and today the world championships attract teams from all over the world. The best players learn to control their breathing, so they don't have to come up for air at a crucial moment of play.

Rules

Played between two teams of six players each, wearing masks, snorkels and fins, the game is in two 15-minute halves. There are three referees, two immersed in the water and one on the pool deck. Fouls, such as taking off an opponent's snorkel or pulling on his or her swimsuit, incur two minutes out of the water.

GREASY POLE

This is a contest that originated in Sicily and is now played by Italian immigrants in parts of the United States. The aim is to grab an Italian flag from the end of a greased, horizontal wooden pole without slipping and falling into the water below. To make the telegraph pole as slippery as possible it is coated with axle grease mixed with Tabasco sauce, laundry detergent and banana peels. Some contestants sprint out as fast as they can in the hope the momentum will carry them forward, while others step out slowly to keep their balance.

Bruises and broken ribs are common and the event sometimes goes on for as long as six or seven rounds, until someone finally manages to capture the flag.

Rules

The pole is 14 metres long (45 feet) and is placed 3.8 metres (10 feet 3 inches) above the water, on a platform protruding about 61 metres (200 feet) from shore. The first person to grab the flag swims to the beach, then parades around the town with the flag on his shoulders.

Champion

Salvi Benson holds the all-time record with 11 wins at the St Peter's Fiesta in Gloucester, Massachusetts.